THIS
DELICIOUS DAY

A RICHARD JACKSON BOOK

OTHER COLLECTIONS
BY PAUL B. JANECZKO

Going Over to Your Place
Pocket Poems
Strings: A Gathering of Family Poems
Poetspeak: In Their Work, About Their Work
Dont Forget to Fly
Postcard Poems

THIS DELICIOUS DAY

65 poems selected by

PAUL B. JANECZKO

ORCHARD BOOKS *New York & London*

A DIVISION OF FRANKLIN WATTS, INC.

ORCHARD BOOKS

387 Park Avenue South
New York, NY 10016

Orchard Books is a division of Franklin Watts, Inc.

Orchard Books Canada
20 Torbay Road
Markham, Ontario 23P 1G6

MANUFACTURED IN THE UNITED STATES OF AMERICA

Book design by Tere LoPrete

10 9 8 7 6 5 4 3 2 1

The text of this book is set in 14 pt. Bodoni Book.

Library of Congress Cataloging-in-Publication Data

Janeczko, Paul B.
This delicious day.

Includes index.
Summary: Sixty-five short poems by a variety of
authors for the funny bone, the sweet tooth, and the
mind's eye.
1. Children's poetry, American. [1. Poetry—
Collections]   I. Title.
PS586.3.J36   1987   811'.008/09282   87-7717
ISBN 0-531-05724-0
ISBN 0-531-08324-1 (lib. bdg.)

With love,
for

R O B

M I C H A E L

C H R I S T O P H E R

E L I Z A B E T H

M A T T H E W

J U L I A

A B B E Y

J E D D

May they and all children live
in a world that allows them to taste
many more delicious days.

Contents

O I Have Dined
on This Delicious Day

O I have dined on this delicious day,
on green-salad treetops wet with beaded
water, tossed by the fork tines of the wind;
devoured the crouton water-birds and
every crumb and crust of the dark-bread earth;
through gristle to the marrowbone of rocks
and the wrinkled grain of high-loaf hills—all
garnished by kindled bush and windrow grass.

O I have bitten into this bright day
and drunk from the clean basin of its sky
till only the clouds were left clinging to
my glass and the sun turned on its spit
into grape-press night and finished with
a frosted melon-ball of yellow moon.

RICHARD   SNYDER

1

In the Morning

In the morning
a little bird
that has no name
flies westward
pulling away
the dark blanket of the night.

SIV CEDERING FOX

In the Shadows of Early Sunlight

At seven, on the dock next door,
   father and son
      clump on the boards, lift
and turn
   a rusty oil-drum
      out of which pour fish (mostly
blues) into a shiny heap.
   They
      hose them down. Seeing
us on our elbows in the window,
   the father calls,
      "Hundred and fifty!"
as the water splashes his trousers.
   We wave.
      We are the first to get the news.

ROBERT WALLACE

Silence

Under a low sky—
this quiet morning
of red and
yellow leaves—
a bird disturbs
no more than one twig
of the green leaved
peach tree

WILLIAM CARLOS WILLIAMS

Bird Theater

At first light
the house cat sits in the window
watching—sparrows mostly,
finches, a jay,
in the various, long leaves of the peach.

Sometimes the mockingbird
with his bag of songs.

Shadowy and musical,
anticipating the peach-colored sun,
they chitter
and hop from limb to limb
in a pageant hours long and fine.

Some have come great distances
to perform for him.

ROBERT WALLACE

6

The Crow

Flying loose and easy, where does he go
Swaggering in the sky, what does he know,
Why is he laughing, the carrion crow?
Why is he shouting, why won't he sing,
How did he steal them, who will he bring
Loaves of blue heaven under each wing?

RUSSELL HOBAN

A Certain Sandpiper

I knew a tiny sandpiper
(Indeed, I know him yet)
Who wrapped his toes in sandpaper
So he wouldn't get them wet.

Now shod in scratchy shoes he goes
To soothe a whale who's stranded,
And he is why the shiny shore
Is always smoothly sanded.

X. J. KENNEDY

8

Cumulus Clouds

a gallon of
rich
country cream

hand-whipped
into stiff
peaks

flung
from the beater

into dollops
across the blue oilcloth

SHERYL L. NELMS

The Loaves

Half a dozen white loaves lie
in the oven of the sky,
round above and flat below.
Who is baking? I don't know;
but, whoever set them there
in the oven of the air,
had better damper down the sun
before the batch is overdone.

RONALD EVERSON

10

Cloud Shadow

A monster
sleeps
on a mountain—
Why?

> A monster
> cloud
> rests
> in the sky.

When the wind
blows,
and the cloud
drifts,

watch—

> below,
> the monster
> shifts,

lifts
its heavy head,

opens
its great paws
and slips away.

LILIAN MOORE

For the Little Girl Who Asked
Why the Kitchen Was So Bright

While you were still asleep
the broom swept all the shadows together.
See how it presses into the corner,
holding the darkness there?

JAMES ULMER

Shadows

Chunks of night
Melt
In the morning sun.
One lonely one
Grows legs
And follows me
To school.

PATRICIA HUBBELL

Stone

Hard, but you can polish it.
Precious, it has eyes. Can wound.
Would dance upon water. Sinks.
Stays put. Crushed, becomes a road.

DONALD JUSTICE

15

Marbles

They are his planets,
his suns and milky spheres, his red Mars.
Their clustered fires seethe in his pocket
till he must touch them, count them
over and over for luck;
aggie and cat's eye, his brilliant clearies,
the prized green shooter
where all the leaves of all his summers burn.
Ambling onto the playground,
he chalks the ring of a universe.
Other boys drift over
to watch a champion set out
marbles like pygmy moons, globes of ice
and crystal, closed worlds
with miniature rivers in them,
colored like sky or tigers, vivid as blood.
It is Genghis Khan baiting his surly chieftains
with hope of treasure,
who hunches beside the circled suns, and aims
that Pearl of Marbles, which obeys
his eye and cunning thumb
so wickedly.

JOAN LaBOMBARD

Bubbles

Two bubbles found they had rainbows on their curves.
They flickered out saying:
"It was worth being a bubble just to have held that rainbow
    thirty seconds."

CARL SANDBURG

17

Alligator Pie

Alligator pie, alligator pie,
If I don't get some I think I'm gonna die.
Give away the green grass, give away the sky,
But don't give away my alligator pie.

Alligator stew, alligator stew,
If I don't get some I don't know what I'll do.
Give away my furry hat, give away my shoe,
But don't give away my alligator stew.

Alligator soup, alligator soup,
If I don't get some I think I'm gonna droop.
Give away my hockey-stick, give away my hoop,
But don't give away my alligator soup.

DENNIS LEE

Fat Lena's Recipe for Crocodile Soup

First, run around in circles
until you drop.
The crocodiles will come
and eat you up.
Then your grandmother
must enter the room
with her ax and chop
the heads off the crocodiles.
She will know how to add water,
salt, pepper, onions and butter
to make a delicious
soup out of them.

PHYLLIS JANOWITZ

19

Arbuckle Jones

Arbuckle Jones
When flustered
Eats custard
With mustard.

I'm disgustard.

PETER WESLEY-SMITH

Celery

Celery, raw,
Develops the jaw,
But celery, stewed,
Is more quietly chewed.

OGDEN NASH

Teresa's Red Adidas
(for T. G.)

I think that I shall never view
Shoes as nice as those on you.
They're red and soft with stripes of white.
One goes left, the other right.
I hope they let you run quick fast;
I also hope they last and last.
Shoes are made for feet like those,
And I just love the ones you chose.

PAUL B. JANECZKO

Shoes

Which to prefer?
Hard leather heels,
Their blocks carved
Thick, like rocks,
Clacked down
Waxed wood stairs,

Or the pale soles
Of sneakers,
Worn smooth, soft
As mushroom caps,
Supple upon warm
Summer pavements?

VALERIE WORTH

Unusual Shoelaces

To lace my shoes
I use spaghetti.
Teacher and friends
All think I'm batty.

Let 'em laugh, the whole
Kit and kaboodle.
But I'll get by.
I use my noodle.

X. J. KENNEDY

Tide and Time

My Aunty Jean
was no mean hortihorologist.
For my fifteenth birthday
she gave me a floral wristwatch.
Wormproof and self-weeding,
its tick was as soft
as a butterfly on tiptoe.

All summer long
I sniffed happily the passing hours.
Until late September
when, forgetting to take it off,
before bathing at New Brighton,
the tide washed time away.

ROGER McGOUCH

In Passing

Open-backed dumpy junktruck
stacked full of old floor-fans,
unplugged, unsteady, undone,
free-whirling like kids' pinwheels
in a last fresh breeze—
What a way to go!

GERALD JONAS

The Chair

A funny thing about a Chair:
You hardly ever think it's *there*.
To know a Chair is really it,
You sometimes have to go and sit.

THEODORE ROETHKE

Mixed-Up School

We have a crazy mixed-up school.
Our teacher Mrs. Cheetah
Makes us talk backwards. Nicer cat
You wouldn't want to meet a.

To start the day we eat our lunch,
Then do some heavy dome-work.
The boys' and girls' rooms go to us,
The hamster marks our homework.

At recess time we race inside
To put on diving goggles,
Play pin-the-donkey-on-the-tail,
Ball-foot or ap-for-bobbles.

Old Cheetah, with a chunk of chalk,
Writes right across two blackbirds,
And when she says, "Go home!" we walk
The whole way barefoot backwards.

X. J. KENNEDY

The Fat Boy

There's a machine
that someday they'll invent
to strip the blubber from his bones.
The fat boy believes
in science and magic.

It's always been like this—
too slow to make the team,
or dance, or even slide on
down the halls like thin ones do.
The girls just look away,
if they look at all.

Fat chance, they say,
which means no chance.
He's burst another sweating seam—
Buddha boy, beached whale,
solitary iceberg that may never melt.
The fat boy believes
in dreams and sighs.

MARK VINZ

29

Blubber Lips

"Blubber Lips, Blubber Lips,
here comes Blubber Lips,"
we taunted Blubber Lips home
from school each day.
His lips like pillows of flesh
stuck out from the unmade bed of his face.
We danced around him, sang our song
as he steady walked silent.
"Blubber Lips, Blubber Lips," every day,
until he punched me in the mouth
and gave me blubber lips
and I learned his real name.

JIM DANIELS

30

The Schoolbus Comes Before the Sun

The day drags by with textbooks
lunch cold and lumpy from a pail
an afternoon of facts
the ride by the nearer farms
where kids get off and horseplay dies
Yarrow bears the rocking of the bus
the fumes   the history teacher's growl
knows there's homework still to do
the sky already dark

Ahead   the mailbox in a drift of snow
the bus is jerking to a stop
Yarrow plunges to the road for home
to Mutt who meets him halfway there
The wiggling dog paws his shoulders
tongue warm and wet to wash away the day

ROBERT CURRIE

Rover

She came out of the field—low
cloud and the land even more dark
where it rolled wide, our farm. She came
limping through our gate into the yard
and up to the door. For greeting, I
held out my hand. I felt the tongue touch
my palm, and a breath came: something
entering my whole life in a rush.

What came to me in trust no one
could take away. I knew
it was mine. Not father, even, or mother,
could end the new feeling: *mine*.
Now I belonged wherever dark
flowed, from that night on,
anywhere, any touch that was kind.

WILLIAM STAFFORD

Early Spring

The dog writes on the window with his nose.

PHILIP WHALEN

Gone

I've looked behind the shed
And under every bed:
I think he must be dead.

What reason for alarm?
He doesn't know the farm.
I *knew* he'd come to harm!

He was a city one
Who never had begun
To think the city fun.

Now where could he have got?
He doesn't know a lot.
I haven't heard a shot.

That old abandoned well,
I thought. Perhaps he fell?
He didn't. I could tell.

Perhaps he found a scent:
A rabbit. Off he went.
He'll come back home all spent.

Groundhogs, they say, can fight;
And raccoons will at night.
He'd not know one by sight!

I've called and called his name.
I'll never be the same.
I blame myself . . . I blame . . .

All *he* knows is the park;
And now it's growing dark.
A bark? You *hear* a bark?

DAVID McCORD

35

Dog's Song

Ants look up as I trot by
and see me passing through the sky.

ROBERT WALLACE

The Gnat

Gnats are gnumerous
But small.
We hardly gnotice them
At all.

EUGENE RUDZEWICZ

Ladybugs

Quarts of ladybugs
scraped off the grapevines
stir and moil in mayonnaise jars.
Here's luck crawling all over itself.

We watch the red and black
kaleidoscope until
grandpa's shoes scrape on the porch
and the screendoor slams.

He squats down
to wirebrush our cheeks,
hums a hum Norwegian.
Still crusted with dirt,
his shoes boom like monster potatoes.

His shoes make things right:
when Lawrence and Welk staggered
and their whiskers lay still in the shoebox,
those shoes walked them out
under the walnut trees
and kicked the shovel into the ground.

But this time they stride
like church shoes
while he shakes the jars,
and takes them outside.

We hear the lids unscrew
and the wings whisper.
He mumbles a few words
and they rise in unison,
a small tornado, that quart of spirit.

PEGGY SHUMAKER

Small, Smaller

I thought that I knew all there was to know
Of being small, until I saw once, black against the snow,
A shrew, trapped in my footprint, jump and fall
And jump again and fall, the hole too deep,
    the walls too tall.

RUSSELL HOBAN

I Wouldn't

There's a mouse house
In the hall wall
With a small door
By the hall floor
Where the fat cat
Sits all day,
Sits that way
All day
Every day
Just to say,
"Come out and play"
To the nice mice
In the mouse house
In the hall wall
With the small door
By the hall floor.

And do they
Come out and play
When the fat cat
Asks them to?

Well, would you?

JOHN CIARDI

41

The Cat Who Aspired to Higher Things

Our cat turns up her nose at mice.
She thinks rhinoceroses
Are twice as nice as mice to chase,
But now the mice are everyplace,

In the furnace,
In the freezer,
In Aunt Edith's orange squeezer,

In the cellar,
In the cider,
In Great-Grandpa's best hang-glider,

In the ginger,
In the allspice,
In Aunt Flora's King Kong false face,

In the stamps,
In the chocolate section
Of my ice cream cone collection—

All four of my uncle Erics
Tear their hair and throw hysterics.
Father smashes chairs and cusses.

At least we've no rhinoceroses.

X. J. KENNEDY

Feline Fine

Tom Tigercat is noted
for his manners and his wit.
He wouldn't think of lion,
no, he doesn't cheetah bit.
Tom never has pretended
to be something that he's not.
I guess that's why we like him
and why he likes ocelot.

J. PATRICK LEWIS

The Two Cats

I'm very good friends with both our cats,
I've know them since they were kittens.
And one is little and one has big paws,
And their names are Midget and Mittens.

But sometimes at dusk when we're driving home
And come on the cats by surprise,
I feel a shiver go down my back
Facing their burning eyes.

ELIZABETH COATSWORTH

When a Cat Is Asleep

When a cat is asleep
There is nothing asleep
That is quite so asleep
As a cat.

She has finished with darting,
Careening and leaping
Now even the soft air around her is sleeping.

KARLA KUSKIN

The Flying Cat

Never, in all your career of worrying, did you imagine
what worries could occur concerning the flying cat.
You are traveling to a distant city.
The cat must travel in a small box with holes.

Will the baggage compartment be pressurized?
Will a soldier's foot-locker fall on the cat during
    take-off?
Will the cat freeze?

You ask these questions one by one, in different voices
over the phone.   Sometimes you get an answer,
sometimes a click.
Now it's affecting everything you do.
At dinner you feel nauseous, like you're swallowing
at twenty thousand feet.
In dreams you wave fish-heads, but the cat has grown
    propellers,
the cat is spinning out of sight!

Will he faint when the plane lands?
Is the baggage compartment soundproofed?
Will the cat go deaf?

"Ma'am, if the cabin weren't pressurized, your cat would
    explode."
And spoken in a droll impersonal voice, as if
the explosion of cats were another statistic!

Hugging the cat before departure, you realize again
the private language of pain.   He purrs.   He trusts you.
He knows little of planets or satellites,
black holes in space or the weightless rise of fear.

NAOMI   SHIHAB   NYE

Feline

Locked up, inside,
I have been watching
spring come on
for weeks now, when
one day my owner
opens the door
and I slip out,
quiet and flat as a shadow.

I am no more than
the slight breath of my passing,
a gust of wind in the grass.
I blend into the hedge
and watch the shrubbery flutter,
the branches crackle and spark.
And oh, I am graceful,
I am sly. Safe
in my leafy disguises,
I watch the day go by.

I am so attentive I can sense
the ants and beetles going on
about their hard business,
the joy of the spirea, dancing,
the dandelions spreading
their delicate messages,
the plum tree conjuring its blossoms.

Now confident and sleek,
I preen from tree to tree, mysterious,
pouring myself out of myself like water.
I am a butterfly, a grass blade, a plum
blossom, a bee; I leap, I shine, I
fly in the dangerous air.
I know I could live here
gentle and fierce forever.

And then, the crows unmask me,
the gray jays cry me naked,
and my owner arrives,
his hands full of promises and pain
and brings me down.
And now we are back in the house,
safe with the tamed oak and maple,
behind these predictable walls,
watching spring angle gracefully
away from us
on its soft impossible paws.

RONALD WALLACE

Mean Rufus Throw-Down

He waits perpetually crouched, teeth,
tongue, raw knuckles, tattooed muscles
bunched under his hide like clouds,
taking and taking and taking until
the right moment tears his eyes open,
his arm, like a lover's curse, snakes
swiftly out to second eating the silky
air of the proudest runner, ending the game.

DAVID SMITH

51

The Hummer

First he drew a strike zone
on the toolshed door, and then
he battered against it all summer
a balding tennis ball, wetted
in a puddle he tended under
an outdoor faucet: that way
he could see, at first, exactly
where each pitch struck.
Late in the game the door
was solidly blotched and
calling the corners was fierce
enough moral work for any
man he might grow up to be.
His stark rules made it hard
to win, and made him finish
any game he started, no matter
if he'd lost it early.
Some days he pitched
six games, the last in dusk,
in tears, in rage, in the blue
blackening joy of obsession.

If he could have been also
the batter, he would have been,
trying to stay alive. Twenty-
seven deaths a game and all
of them his. For a real game
the time it takes is listed
in the boxscore, the obituary.
What he loved was mowing
them down. Thwap. Thwap.
Then one thwap low and outside.
And finally the hummer.
It made him grunt to throw it,
as if he'd tried to hold it
back, but it escaped. Thwap.

WILLIAM MATTHEWS

Nothing But Net

The jump shot? It's all in the wrist
and follow-through, and the timing
of the jump. Of course it's one thing
to hit one in a game of HORSE,
and something else over a guy
that's guarding you. What I like best
is shooting baskets by myself,
warming up gradually until,
at the very height of my jump,
I can tell that it's going in
as the ball leaves my fingertips,
arcing to intercept the air
at the dead center of the goal—
that one split second of eclipse.

ROY SCHEELE

54

Shooting

Dusk was best. Searching
for the perfect shot,
I'd dribble, pivot, jump,
let go, and watch the ball
float full-moon across
a darkening sky, then sink
into the strings that hugged,
then dropped it to the ground.
Far into the night
I stayed, moving through
the backyard gloom, a ghost
even to myself, shooting
where I couldn't see.
The sounds of bounce and jump
echoed from the house,
followed by the silence
of the ball's long flight.

Going up, each time
my body felt itself
curve evenly from toe
to shoulder, through arms
and fingertips that sensed
the arc the ball would take
before the quick whisper
somewhere in the dark.

B. H. FAIRCHILD

Zimmer's Street

My street thunders like
A long chimney falling
When morning comes up.
A thousand great cars
Relentlessly flash and fume.
Trucks come, an ambulance,
A wrecking ball and crane,
A hearse, cabs, a mobile home,
Airplanes roar and stack above
My father and mother going to work.
My wife and children
Play on the sidewalks,
Grandfather walks to
The bakery, my older sister
Bounces a ball till dark.
All things have come down
This street: Thanksgiving,
Christmas, victory, marriage.
It takes all day for
The pavement to stop hissing
So that I can sleep at night.

PAUL ZIMMER

57

Mother

My mother says
If the neighbor boys
Keep having quarrels
And making noise,
She'll surely jump right out of her skin.
But I say, "Don't,"
And I hope she won't
Unless she's able to jump back in.

KATE STARBIRD

Real Talent

Dad had some
talent

he could stand on
his head

he would make
that prefect tripod
then slowly
precisely
raise
his legs

then there he was

all six foot two
of him
upside down

smiling

SHERYL L. NELMS

Kate and I

Days when fir trees reared and shook
Like great polar bears emerging
From the ice blocked sea,
My sister Kate and I
Would launch forth on our sleds
To skim the rapids of the snow
And reap the windfall drifts.

Or once when the noon sun
Had flayed the ice from the sled track,
We turned Eskimo,
And sought deep snow on the lee side of hills.

Wallowing heavy footed in galoshes,
We strained against the trammels
Of our snow suits like huskies,
And rolled ponderous spheres to make an igloo.

We planed the inner walls with our slick mittens
And dug out a pantry for winter preserves,
Then like seals, we popped from the entrance hole,
Our noses powdered finely in white,
And stood to watch for herds of caribou,
Or enemy kyacks advancing from the east.

SUSAN NAVARRE TARRANT

60

My Brother Flies Over Low

Nobody could believe
my brother ever got through
that pilot school in Texas
because it was well known
in town he couldn't drive
a car worth a damn. So he'd
made a point of wearing his
uniform whenever he came
home and telling people
to watch out for him, he
was going to fly over low
one of these days. Which
he did, he and a buddy also
stationed down in Goldsboro,
made 2 passes, each one sounding
like 14 freight trains
falling off a cliff, waggled
their wings and headed on back
down to North Carolina,
gaining altitude as they went.

Mother was hanging out a wash,
and Mary King was coming up
the hill to help her with
spring cleaning, and they say
Miss Ossie Price came running
out of her store to see what
was the matter. And nobody
sees my brother now but what
they grin at him, shake their
heads and say something like,
"Great God Almighty, Bill."
Mother won't talk about it
in public, claims to be
embarrassed about the whole
thing, but she doesn't fool
anybody.

DAVID HUDDLE

In the Music

Yarrow liked it
when his uncles came
the house a sounding board
around their instruments
He lay upon the chesterfield
let the hours go humming by
till someone thought of clocks
remembering him
and sent him off to bed

Beneath the frosted rafters
he pulled the quilt up to his chin
shivered with the welcome chill
let the music wash him
tumbling in the waves of song
floating easy on a sound
he rode his uncle's fiddle bow
into the warming dawn

ROBERT CURRIE

Concert

When Aunt Wessie played she
reached into the keys with heavy
arms as though rooting tomato
slips, sinking hands in to

the wrists and raking the dirt
smooth, humming as she worked.
Would awaken suddenly from her reverie
and plunge onto the keyboard jamming the

pedal in like an accelerator
and slapping chords over
the melody till
the whole room filled

and beat like a sounding board
and every note on the trellis of wires blurred.
Almost blind, she stayed alone
in her house on the mountain

while we worked off in the fields.
As her hearing failed
the TV blasted soap tragedy
all over the valley.

ROBERT MORGAN

64

Aunt Leaf

Needing one, I invented her—
the great-great-aunt dark as hickory
called Shining-Leaf, or Drifting-Cloud
or The-Beauty-of-the-Night.

Dear aunt, I'd call into the leaves,
and she'd rise up, like an old log in a pool,
and whisper in a language only the two of us knew
the word that meant *follow*,

and we'd travel
cheerful as birds
out of the dusty town and into the trees
where she would change us both into something quicker—
two foxes with black feet,
two snakes green as ribbons,
two shimmering fish—
and all day we'd travel.

At day's end she'd leave me back at my own door
with the rest of my family,
who were kind, but solid as wood
and rarely wandered. While she,
old twist of feathers and birch bark,
would walk in circles wide as rain and then
float back

scattering the rags of twilight
on fluttering moth wings;

or she'd slouch from the barn like a gray opossum;

or she'd hang in the milky moonlight
burning like a medallion,

this bone dream,
this friend I had to have,
this old woman made out of leaves.

M A R Y   O L I V E R

Sunset

There's dazzle
     in the western sky,
colors spill and
     run.
The pond mouth
lies open
     greedy
for the last drop
of
melting
sun.

LILIAN MOORE

Dusk

Dusk over the lake,
clouds floating,
heat lightning
a nightmare behind branches;
from the swamp
the odor of cedar and fern,
the long circular
wail of the loon—
the plump bird aches for fish
for night to come down.

Then it becomes so dark
and still
that I shatter the moon with an oar.

JAMES HARRISON

68

The Beach at Evening

The beach at this evening full
Tide is a fisherman's back,
Whose bright muscles of rock
Glisten and strain as they pull
The cast net of the sea
In with a full catch
Of pebble, shell, and other
Things that belong to the sea.

DAVID FERRY

Evening Tide

Darkness invades the shallows of the street.
A tricycle left outdoors starts nodding and bobbing.

On its recliner by dusk set afloat
Father's head lolls, its dome of beer half-emptied.

Under the parked car in the driveway, shadows seep
And somewhere the cry of a child protesting bed
Comes blundering in again and again, a stick of driftwood.

X. J. KENNEDY

70

Stars

At dusk the first stars appear.
Not one eager finger points toward them.
A little later the stars spread with the night
And an orange moon rises
To lead them, like a shepherd, toward dawn.

GARY SOTO

Rags

The night wind
rips a cloud sheet
into rags,

then rubs, rubs
the October moon
until it shines
like a brass doorknob.

JUDITH THURMAN

Night Crawler

Night crawler,
night crawler,
poor little creep,
don't crawl about now
but go home and sleep.
Crawl into bed now
and don't stay up late.
Late night crawlers
end up as bait.

N. M. BODECKER

Song for Susannah: A Lullaby

All the sun's peacocks are dreaming.
They have gathered their colors
and gone screaming to sleep,
swept up green shining gold
and a thousand indigo hearts
like cards when the game is done.

See how the day has grown weary.
It is an ancient gray man
taken to wandering
who shuffles his feet
and wears a ragged red sun
on a stick.

Do you not think that tomorrow will come?
Oh look, silly girl, how the birds have grown still
and the moon has wept frost on the leaves.

DORIS HARDIE

Lullaby
(after Atila Josef)

Sweet love, everything
closes its eyes now to sleep.
The cat
          has stretched out
at the foot of your bed
& the little bug
               lays its head
in its arms
& your jacket
that's draped on the chair:
every button has fallen asleep,
even the poor torn cuff . . .
                    & your flute
& your paper boat
& the candy bar
               snug in its wrapper.
Outside,
the evening is closing its eyes.
Even the hill to the dark
woods
has fallen asleep
on its side
          in a quilt of blue snow.

STEVE KOWIT

75

Past

I have all these parts   stuffed in
                                   me
like mama's chicken
                  and
            biscuits,
                  and
daddy's apple pie, and a tasty
                              story
from the family
            tree.
But I know that tomorrow
                  morning
      I'll wake up
            empty, and hungry for that
                                    next
                              bite
      of my new
            day

ARNOLD ADOFF

Acknowledgments

Permission to reprint copyrighted poems is gratefully acknowledged to the following:

Angus & Robertson (UK) Ltd. for "Arbuckle Jones" from *The Ombley-Gombley* by Peter Wesley-Smith.

Atheneum Publishers, Inc. for "Night Crawler" from *Hurry, Hurry, Mary Dear! and Other Nonsense Poems* by N. M. Bodecker, copyright © 1976 by N. M. Bodecker (A Margaret K. McElderry Book); for "Stone" from "Things" in *Departures* by Donald Justice, copyright © 1973 by Donald Justice; for "Sunset" from *Sam's Place* (1973) in the compilation *Something New Begins* by Lilian Moore, copyright © 1982 by Lilian Moore; and for "Rags" from *Flashlight and Other Poems* by Judith Thurman, copyright © 1976 by Judith Thurman.

The Basilisk Press for "Mean Rufus Throw-Down" from *Mean Rufus Throw-Down* by David Jeddie Smith, copyright © 1973 by David Jeddie Smith.

Georges Borchardt for "The Gnat" by Eugene Rudzewicz from *A Child's Bestiary* by John Gardner, copyright © 1977 by Boskydell Artists, Ltd.

Jonathan Cape Ltd. for "Time and Tide" by Roger McGough from *Holiday on Death Row* by Roger McGough.

Carcanet Press Limited for "Silence" from *Collected Later Poems* by William Carlos Williams.

Carnegie-Mellon University Press for "Bird Theater" and "Dog's Song" from *Swimmer in the Rain* by Robert Wallace, copyright © 1979 by Robert Wallace.

Carpenter Press for "Lullaby" from *Lurid Impressions* by Steve Kowit, copyright © 1983 by Steve Kowit.

Colbert Agency, Inc. for "Alligator Pie" by Dennis Lee, copyright © 1974 by Dennis Lee.

Curtis Brown, Ltd. for "Mixed-Up School" and "Unusual Shoelaces" from *One Winter Night* by X. J. Kennedy, copyright © 1975 by X. J. Kennedy and "The Cat Who Aspired to Higher Things" and "A Certain Sandpiper" from *The Phantom Ice Cream Machine* by X. J. Kennedy, copyright © 1975, 1977, 1978, 1979 by X. J. Kennedy; and for "Celery" from *Good Intentions* by Ogden Nash, copyright © 1942 in the United Kingdom.

Jim Daniels for "Blubber Lips," copyright © 1986 by Jim Daniels.

Doubleday & Company, Inc. for "The Chair" from *The Collected Poems of Theodore Roethke* by Theodore Roethke, copyright © 1950 by Theodore Roethke.

Roger Everson for "The Loaves" from *The Wind Has Wings: Poems from Canada*, edited by Mary Alice Downie and Barbara Robertson (Henry Z. Walck, Publishers).

Faber and Faber, Ltd. for "The Chair" from *The Collected Poems of Theodore Roethke* by Theodore Roethke.

B. H. Fairchild for "Shooting."

Farrar, Straus and Giroux, Inc. for "Shoes" from *More Small Poems* by Valerie Worth, copyright © 1976 by Valerie Worth.

David R. Godine Publisher, Inc. for "Evening Tide" from *Emily Dickinson in Southern California* by X. J. Kennedy, copyright © 1973 by X. J. Kennedy.

80

81

Index of Poets